Map Workbook

for

WESTERN CIVILIZATION

VOLUME II

Cynthia Kosso
Northern Arizona University

Wadsworth
Thomson Learning™

Australia • Canada • Mexico • Singapore • Spain • United Kingdom • United States

For permission to use material from this text,
contact us by **Web**: http://wwwthomsonrights.com
Fax: 1-800-730-2215 **Phone:** 1-800-730-2214

ISBN 0-534-56845-9

For more information, contact
Wadsworth/Thomson Learning
10 Davis Drive
Belmont, CA 94002-3098
USA
http://www.wadsworth.com

International Headquarters
Thomson Learning
International Division
290 Harbor Drive, 2nd Floor
Stamford, CT 06902-7477
USA

UK/Europe/Middle East/South Africa
Thomson Learning
Berkshire House
168-173 High Holborn
London WC1V 7AA
United Kingdom

Asia
Thomson Learning
60 Albert Complex, #15-01
Singapore 189969

Canada
Nelson Thomson Learning
1120 Birchmount Road
Toronto, Ontario M1K 5G4
Canada

Contents

Notes

Introduction

Map reading is an important part of any person's basic knowledge about the world, whether for travel or keeping track of events around the world.[1] When someone gives you directions, or asks them of you, your brain automatically attempts to draw a rudimentary map. Your mind may even see roads as lines and rivers as bands or buildings as small squares. Maps are, of course, also useful for understanding history and geography. Maps tell us about the physical and cultural aspects of the world—and they can be deceiving. Colors and size can be used subtly to suggest "good guys" or "bad guys," or relative importance. In addition, maps have a long and interesting history.

A Brief History of Maps

Old maps and prints are fascinating because of their power to reflect the history of the world. When and where the very first maps were created is unknown. But clearly as soon as symbols were used, people felt the need to draw routes and illustrate their own territories. Among the earliest of known maps was one found in Turkey (Anatolia) at the site of Çatal Hüyük, dating to about 6300 BCE. This map, a wall painting, is a town plan, with a volcano looming in the background. Egyptians, Assyrians, and Babylonians also produced early maps and plans on papyrus and clay tablets. These were most likely land surveys for tax purposes. Controversy concerning the shape of the earth consumed philosophers from Anaximander to Strabo. Determining the shape of the earth, its size, habitable areas, climate zones and relative positions of regions preoccupied mapmakers over the centuries. Mathematicians, philosophers, and astronomers all sought answers to these problems. Plato, Herodotus, and Aristotle thought the world was round, an idea that eventually took hold in the Hellenic world. From our point of view, Strabo plays an important role in preserving the story of early map developments, though he misinterpreted the calculations made by Eratosthenes and Posidonius concerning the circumference of the earth. His work, *Geography*, is preserved in eight books and reveals sound geographic understanding. It also reveals an encyclopedic understanding of the countries and people of the Mediterranean region.

The Greek mathematician, Claudius Ptolemy, produced one of the most important early developments in map making. In ca. 150 CE, he collated all known information and

---

[1] I would like to thank the undergraduate students in the History of Western Civilization courses at Northern Arizona University. They provided indispensable help and advice in the development of my workbooks. I would also like to thank Kevin and Arthur Lawton for their editorial and content advice.

created his own *Geography* (another work in eight volumes). This work became the basis of mapping for about the next 1000 years and influenced the mapmakers who provided maps for explorers such as Columbus, Cabot, and Magellan. However, improvements in map making were slowed by the fall of the Roman Empire and the loss or dissipation of accumulated information. Increasing religious piety, and the belief in a flat world, forced the simplification of maps in Western Europe.

Following the Crusades, westerners were reintroduced to Ptolemy's work as well as the sophisticated mathematical knowledge of the Arabs which, fortunately, influenced later medieval mapmakers. Greek manuscripts from Constantinople were brought west, and once translated into Latin, began to intrigue scholars of historical geography. With the advent of printing, the production of numerous copies of maps became possible. The "age of discovery" brought more than discoveries of new lands—it brought the discovery of new geometric methods of survey and the invention of better instruments. Increasingly modern and recognizable maps were made. The Spanish and the Portuguese were particularly influential because of their fine early maritime charts (although, of course, at first these were kept very secret). In 1569, after advances in surveying technology had been made, the first Mercator maps were produced. As the quality of maps improved, they became art forms in their own right. Still, they contained numerous inaccuracies—California, for example, was drawn as an island.

During the 18th century the demand for maps grew stronger and both the middle classes and elites collected atlases, maps, new books, and similar luxuries. Many of these were huge folio maps, highly decorated. It was this elite market that began to demand more accuracy in map making, ultimately to the benefit of all. With the invention of steel engraving in the 19th century, mass production of maps became even easier. Maps were printed in large quantities and it was easier to keep them up to date. However, with an increase in accuracy, decoration became less common—slowly maps lost most of their decorative features as can be seen in modern maps, such as those in this workbook and in your atlases and texts. Aerial photography and satellite surveying have helped to furnish a wealth of detail hitherto missing from maps and these techniques have been used to enhance the accuracy and detail of all kinds of maps.

Defining Maps

In a way, maps are very simple. They are just a geographic region drawn on a flat surface. Typically, there are a number of commonly accepted standards and symbols used by all modern mapmakers. These symbols are defined in a key. In order to make the map (or to read one), a frame of reference is chosen. Within the frame of reference, a grid system, created by drawing the lines of latitude and longitude, helps to pinpoint locations accurately. Mapmakers chose the north and south poles as two definite, not arbitrary, points from which to begin dividing the world. Midway between these poles a line was drawn around the world (this is the equator). Next, lines were drawn parallel to the equator and moving toward each of the poles (the lines of **latitude**). To complete the grid, lines were drawn from pole to pole (the lines of **longitude**).

While the equator provides a natural line from which to measure, there is no such natural longitude line (although one was put in by convention and is called the **prime meridian**). A longitudinal starting point is obviously needed as a point of reference. The line through Greenwich, England is now most commonly used, but many nations have created maps with their own most important cities as reference points. The United States made maps with Washington, D.C., as the prime meridian. The Spanish drew their reference line through Madrid, the Greeks through Athens, the Dutch through Amsterdam, and so on.

Maps are designed with different scales—different proportions, or ratios, between the distance on the map and the actual distance on the world. The larger the fraction (or **proportion**), the smaller the territory covered. Inches per mile or centimeters per kilometer are the most common kind of **scale**. The scale is merely a fraction comparing the measures on the map (inches or centimeters) with the measures on the ground (miles or kilometers).

Finding the exact location of any place requires several steps. Reproducing the location accurately is complicated by the unavoidable distortion that arises from representing as a spatially flat surface, a region that lies on a round world. You may notice that the shapes of continents change slightly from map to map. This is because the distortion differs with the perspective of the map. Obviously, flat maps are not likely to be completely superseded by globes. Carrying a globe on a hike or road trip would be very inconvenient.

Map projections are the various ways in which one deals with the problem of distortion on a map of the earth's surface. The world is round. The map page is flat. All mapmakers, therefore, pick a perspective and a scale from which to display their particular purpose or orientation. For a map nearly devoid of distortion, one must have a spherical surface (this is known as a **globe**). Obviously, a flat map cannot perfectly represent a round surface. Typically a compromise is made whereby the directions, distances, and areas are drawn with the least inaccuracy possible to each. The **Mercator** maps are an example of how this works. The Mercator projection (as seen in the example above) is related to a cylindrical projection—that is, the mapmaker, or cartographer, works with the map as though it were a cylinder that circles the globe. Mercator maps, therefore, show the equator with great accuracy, while they distort the highest latitudes (this is known as the "Greenland problem").

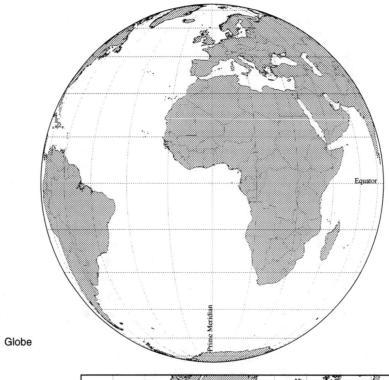

Globe

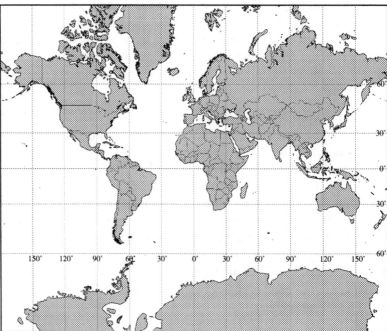

Mercator Projection

Map Perspectives

There are, as well, several kinds of maps. Hydrographic charts, used for navigation, show bodies of water and shores. Geologic maps show the physical structure of a region, while topographic maps show man-made and natural surface features in given regions. Political maps (as in the map of Europe below) traditionally show territorial boundaries and political divisions.

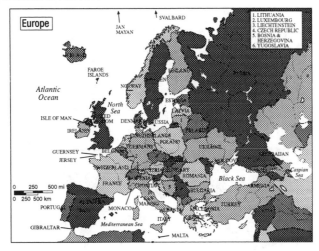

Political Europe

Climate maps (as seen in a climate map of Europe shown below) indicate the climates of various regions.

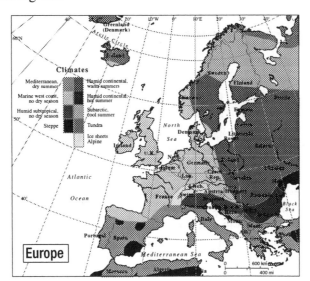

Europe Climate

And population maps (as seen below in the example showing the population of Europe) describe the distribution of numbers of people among regions.

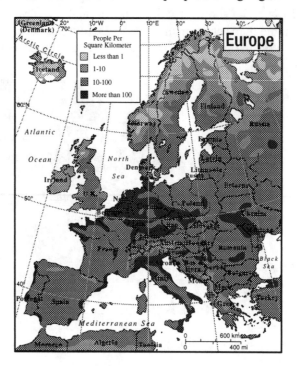

Europe Population

Every map, therefore, has a particular perspective. It has an author (the cartographer), a subject, and a theme. The subject in this exercise book is Western Civilization; themes vary from boundaries to distribution of religious groups. The subject and theme represent the author's interest, skills, political viewpoints, and historical context. Thus, maps represent only a version of reality. Maps are like snapshots of the world, a moment in time and space with a definite historical context. A nice example of perspective can be seen in one of the earliest maps known from the Babylonians. In this map, the Babylonians are situated precisely in the middle of the universe; all territories radiated from them—their own perception of the world.

A world map from the 16th century shows the continents as the Europeans knew them during this age of discovery. Compare a 16th century map to any later chart of the Americas and note how different in size and shape the continents are at different periods of time (clearly, the continents themselves did not change that much that quickly). The earlier world map reveals not only the author's knowledge of geography, but his interests—as indicated by the details he chose to include.

x

Still, in the search for accuracy and objectivity, one simply cannot add all details in all maps; the map would be rendered incomprehensibly complicated and useless. Nevertheless, maps are becoming increasingly accurate. Cartographers, especially since the late Middle Ages, have worked to perfect map making.

This map exercise book is designed to clarify the relationships among places and people through time—to help you to order events and historical locations. All sections incorporate several parts. Location sections ask you to find and correctly place a city, site, or other feature, or draw a boundary. Geography or environment sections require you to become familiar with the natural contours and context of a region. The human society and civilization sections ask you interpret human interactions with other civilizations and with the natural world. You will need to discuss and synthesize historical and geographical information in short essays. This workbook is intended to aid you in the study and understanding of how events, people, and natural processes relate to one another temporally.

Bibliography

Demko, George with Jerome Agel and Eugene Boe. 1992. *Why in the World, Adventures in Geography*. New York: Doubleday. This is a fun and easy to read introduction to mapping and geography. It does an excellent job of pointing out the importance of geography.

Greenhood, David. 1964. *Mapping*. Chicago: University of Chicago Press. This book provides a clear and concise introduction to maps and mapping.

Harley, J. B. and D. Woodward (eds.), *The History of Cartography*, University of Chicago Press (in press). Present the history of maps and mapping in several volumes.

Talbert, Richard J. A., "Mapping the Classical World: Major Atlases and Map Series 1872–1990," *Journal of Roman Archaeology* 5 (1992: 5-38. This article is especially interesting for students of ancient history.

Wood, Denis. 1992. *The Power of Maps*. New York: The Guilford Press. In this book Wood shows how maps are used and abused. It is an excellent introduction to the way maps have been used by groups and individuals to make an argument or present a point of view.

Useful Web Sites

http://www.pcclinics.com/maps/hist_sites.htm
http://www.maps.com

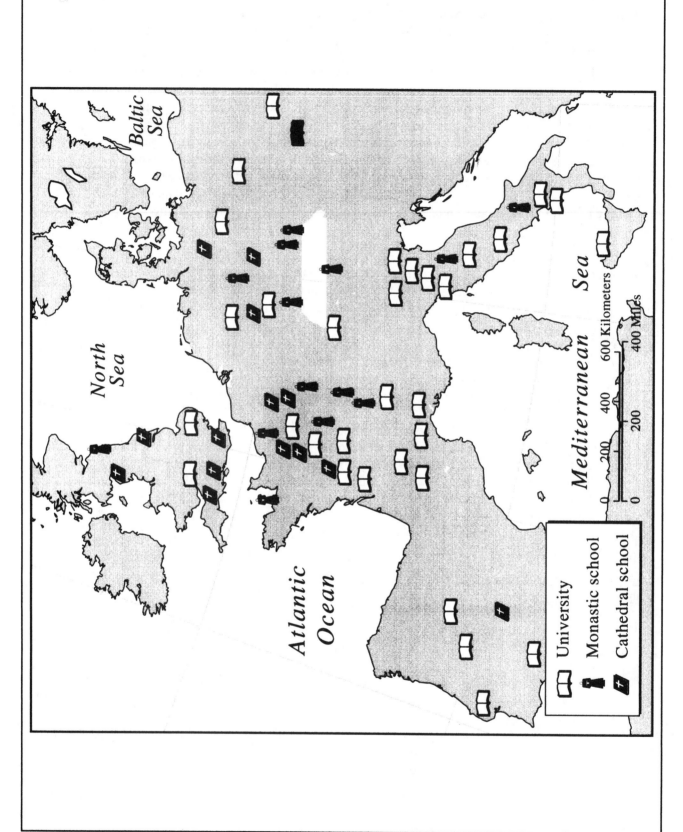

Baltic Sea

North Sea

Atlantic Ocean

Mediterranean Sea

University
Monastic school
Cathedral school

600 Kilometers
400 Miles
200   400
0   200   400

MAP 7

Part Three: Late Middle Ages to the Reformation

The 12th through the 16th centuries saw a myriad of rapid, and profoundly influential, developments. Technological transformations, the creation of universities, population fluctuations and the infusion of dramatically new ideas led to the foundations of modern religious divisions and systems of government. There were a variety of reasons for these changes, including but not limited to, new ways of thinking imported from the east though peaceful trade and the violence of the Crusades, dislocations caused by the Black Death, (which was a disaster of enormous magnitude), and conflicts within and surrounding the Catholic church.

The Spread of New Ideas: Education

Intellectual life in the later Middle Ages reflected a period of exceptional vitality and change. The clergy, hitherto the main educators in the European world, began to lose some of their dominance and influences in education began to be felt from the work of secular officials, warriors, courtiers, philosophers and aristocrats. The university, in its modern form, developed during this era in order to train both an educated clergy and educated secular citizenry.

Locations

On Map 7, place the appropriate city center next to its university, monastic school, or cathedral school icon.

1.	Bologna	6.	Naples	11.	Reims
2.	Cambridge	7.	Notre Dame	12.	Rome
3.	Chartres	8.	Oxford	13.	Seville
4.	Durham	9.	Paris	14.	Toledo
5.	Mainz	10.	Prague	15.	Vienna

Society and Civilization

1. Briefly, list five of the earliest major Universities with the date of their foundation.

_____

_____

_____

_____

_____

2. What were the origins of these schools? Why did schools arise in the locations that they did?

_____

_____

_____

_____

_____

_____

_____

_____

3. What physical and educational characteristics did these early universities share?

_____

_____

_____

_____

_____

4. Can you explain why there were fewer universities in Spain than in France?

_____

_____

_____

_____

_____

5. What effect did the humanist movement have on education and the locations of schools?

_____

_____

_____

_____

_____

Life In A Medieval University

6.   Imagine that you are a student in Bologna. Write a letter to your father describing your location and experiences.

_____

_____

_____

_____

_____

_____

_____

_____

_____

_____

_____

_____

_____

_____

_____

_____

_____

_____

_____

_____

_____

_____

_____

_____

_____

_____

_____

_____

_____

_____

_____

_____

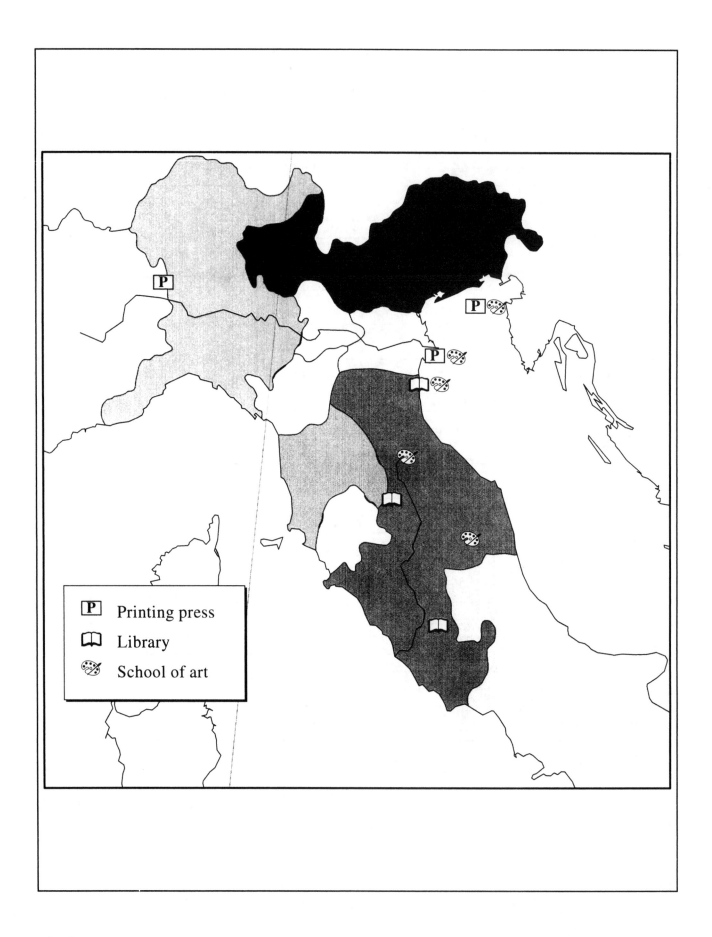

P   Printing press

   Library

   School of art

MAP 8

Culture and Politics: Italy and the Renaissance

State systems varied by region and era. For example, though in the fourteenth century Italy had a well-established system of city-state governments, often in conflict with one another, by the fifteenth century there were only a few, very powerful states left. They vied with one another for a variety of reasons, often calling on the Papacy or the Holy Roman Empire of the Germans to support their claims. Frequent warfare was the result, and unification of nations such as Italy was a long way away. Europe had entered a period of turmoil and rebirth exemplified by political rivalries as well as intellectual and artistic achievements of the Renaissance and Reformation.

Locations

On Map 8, next to the symbols for presses, libraries, and schools of art, write the name of the associated city. In the proper area, also write in the following regions:

Duchy of Ferarra	Papal States
Duchy of Milan	Republic of Florence
Duchy of Modena	Republic of Lucca
Duchy of Savoy	Republic of Siena
Kingdom of Naples	Republic of Venice

Culture And Society

1. How did the five major 15th-century powers in Italy come to dominance?

_____

_____

_____

_____

_____

_____

_____

_____

2.   What role did geography play in the development of these regional powers?

_____
_____
_____
_____
_____
_____
_____
_____

3.   Compare and contrast the Renaissance of Italy and the Northern Renaissance. In what ways were these "rebirths" most similar and in what ways were they most different?

_____
_____
_____
_____
_____
_____
_____
_____
_____

4.   How did geography and location affect regional developments? Be specific.

_____
_____
_____
_____
_____
_____
_____
_____

5.   Using Renaissance recipes and menus as guides, discuss how trade in Renaissance Italy affected the daily lives of the elite.

_____
_____
_____
_____
_____
_____
_____

Politics and Religion: The Reformation

In contrast to Italy, Spain was home to several independent Christian nations that had managed, militarily, to take the peninsula from those practicing Islam and Judaism. The Spanish enforced strict orthodoxy. Unlike the leaders and states of Italy, Isabella of Castile and Ferdinand of Aragon made major progress toward early unification of the Iberian Peninsula. Their combined power and wealth, plus the support of the Catholic Church would make them a real threat to countries near and far. Yet, at the same time the Christian church in the sixteenth century was suffering from the consequences of abuses by Catholics (in particular the papacy) and was reaching a crisis point. Many reform movements grew out of the frustration of the times; some made surprisingly influential by the dissemination of these new ideas through the written word, now easily spread because of the printing press. The Reformation in Germany led by Martin Luther was to be one of the most influential. It was not long before the populations of Europe had chosen sides: Protestant (e.g., Lutheran, Calvinist, Anglican) or Catholic.

1.   Compare and contrast the Reformation in England and Germany. How did local conditions affect the different approaches to reformation?

_____
_____
_____
_____
_____
_____
_____
_____

2.   What impact did the Reformation generally have on the economy of Europe? Give several examples.

_____
_____
_____
_____
_____
_____
_____

45

3.   What impact did the Reformation have on the political life and territorial boundaries of Europe? And, on the other hand, what impact did existing territorial divisions have on the progress of the Reformation?

_____
_____
_____
_____
_____
_____
_____
_____
_____

4.   What impact did the Reformation have on the society of Europe? Give several examples.

_____
_____
_____
_____
_____
_____
_____
_____

5.   Next to the following cities, list the appropriate religious affiliation (Anglican, Calvinist, Calvinist influenced, Roman Catholic, Lutheran, Lutheran influenced).

A.   Amsterdam   _____

B.   Cologne   _____

C.   Dijon   _____

D.   Edinburgh   _____

E.   Geneva   _____

F.   London   _____

G.   Madrid   _____

H. Oxford   _____

I. Paris   _____

J. Rome   _____

K. Seville   _____

L. Trent   _____

M. Vienna   _____

N. Wittenberg   _____

O. Worms   _____

Life and Death in the Middle Ages

The Black Death killed from 25 to 50% of the population of Europe. In some cases, entire villages were wiped out. Some cities saw their populations reduced by more than half. The disaster had cultural, economic and religious results.

6.   Briefly describe the nature of the Black Death and outline its progress through Europe.

_____

_____

_____

_____

_____

_____

_____

_____

7.   How did the environment of Europe influence the progress of the Black Death?

_____

_____

_____

_____

_____

_____

_____

_____

8. Discuss European responses to the Black Death. What were some of the psychological and religious responses experienced by the inhabitants of Europe? Give specific examples.

_____
_____
_____
_____
_____
_____
_____
_____
_____
_____
_____

9. What economic ramifications did the Black Death have? Be detailed.

_____
_____
_____
_____
_____
_____
_____
_____
_____
_____
_____

10. In what ways did the Black Death have long term political effects?

_____
_____
_____
_____
_____
_____
_____
_____
_____
_____

Late Middle Ages to the Reformation: Test Your Knowledge

Next to the name listed below, list the individual's date, major achievements or characteristics, and main location of activity:

1.   Botticelli, Sandro

_____

_____

_____

_____

2.   Charles V (Holy Roman Emperor)

_____

_____

_____

_____

3.   da Vinci, Leonardo

_____

_____

_____

_____

4.   della Mirandola, Pico

_____

_____

_____

5.   di Donatello, Donato

_____

_____

_____

_____

6.   Dufay, Guillaume

_____

_____

_____

_____

_____

_____

7.   Erasmus, Desiderius

_____

_____

_____

_____

_____

_____

8.   Gutenberg, Johannes

_____

_____

_____

_____

_____

_____

9.   Henry VIII

_____

_____

_____

_____

_____

_____

10. Hus, John

_____

_____

_____

_____

_____

_____

11. Isabella of Castile

_____

12. King Louis XI of France

_____

13. Loyola, Ignatius

_____

14. Luther, Martin

_____

15. Michelangelo

_____

16. More, Thomas

_____

_____

_____

_____

_____

_____

17. Pope Paul III

_____

_____

_____

_____

_____

_____

_____

18. Prince Ivan III

_____

_____

_____

_____

_____

19. Raphael

_____

_____

_____

_____

20. Zwingli, Ulrich

_____

_____

_____

_____

_____

Part Four: Early Modern Europe

After the Reformation swept Europe a system of secular states began to appear. Absolutist monarchs tried to stabilize the boundaries and societies of the European states. After the end of the Thirty Years' War, however, Germany was still made up of more than three hundred independent states, each vying for power and territory. The Holy Roman Empire was an entity in name only. Out of the hundreds of German states, two became most powerful: Brandenburg and Austria. Both of these states would grow and strengthen because of particularly dominating families, the Hohenzollerns and the Hapsburgs respectively. Political change led to local disruptions and rebellions.

Expansion, Crises, and Enlightenment

In 1492, a new era in world history was launched. European adventurers took their ships in search of wealth, fame and new worlds to conquer and convert. These men provoked a transformation of Africa, Asia, the America's and Europe itself. A ferment of ideas and scientific advances furthered European efforts to explore and dominate the entire world. The English, French, Spanish, Portuguese and Dutch all fanned out to conquer and colonize the old and New World. Discoveries and conquests of rich and unusual lands and people kept Europeans interested in the foreign travel and control. Settlements and ports were founded along the coasts of Africa. Across the Atlantic, the Spanish especially, established rich and vast empires, conquering and killing huge numbers of Amerindians in the process, and then replacing these indigenous people with imported slave laborers from Africa.

Back at home, divine-right kings dominated European states in the 16th century. Cultural and political differences remained, however, and these led to very different forms of government as the centuries passed. England, for example, eventually created a constitutional monarchy, while France was ruled, absolutely, by the "Sun King" from his magnificent palace at Versailles.

Yet the ideals of the Enlightenment were professed by all alike: constitutional as well as absolute monarchs. Austria was ruled by an "enlightened" monarch who tried hard to reform government and, in particular, tried to limit the power of the Catholic Church.

Peter the Great, and then, Catherine the Great of Russia, likewise tried to turn toward the west's ideas of enlightened rule and at the same time use the west for trade and technology.

ℰ𝒫

Politics and Place

1.   List and give the dates for the main voyages of discovery in the 15th and 16th centuries.

A. _____

B. _____

C. _____

D. _____

E. _____

F. _____

G. _____

H. _____

I. _____

2.   What territories in the New World were under Spanish control by the 16th century?

_____

_____

_____

_____

_____

_____

_____

3.   What territories were under Portuguese control by the 16th century?

_____

_____

_____

_____

_____

_____

_____

4. How were the New World territories administrated?

_____

_____

_____

_____

_____

_____

_____

5. What problems arose in the new territories because of the vast distances to the homelands?

_____

_____

_____

_____

_____

_____

6. Write an essay discussing the short and long-term impact of European settlement on the people and environment of the New World. What impact did the discovery of these territories have on the countries and people of Europe?

_____

_____

_____

_____

_____

_____

_____

_____

_____

_____

_____

_____

_____

_____

_____

_____

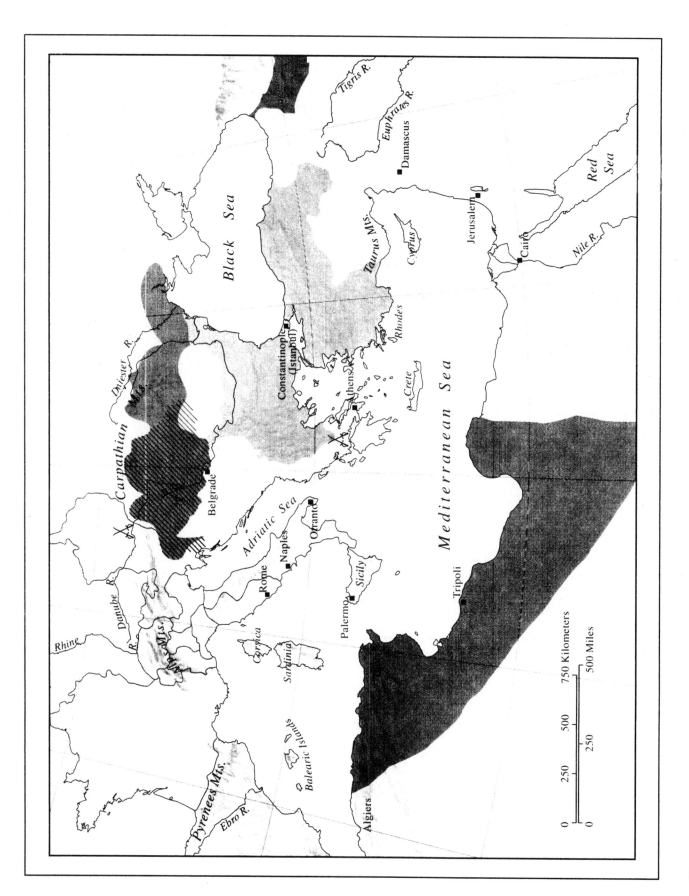

Black Sea

Tigris R.

Euphrates R.

Damascus

Red Sea

Jerusalem

Cairo

Nile R.

Taurus Mts.

Cyprus

Mediterranean Sea

Rhodes

Constantinople
(Istanbul)

Athens

Crete

Dniester R.

Carpathian Mts.

Belgrade

Adriatic Sea

Otranto

Naples

Rome

Sicily

Palermo

Tripoli

Danube R.

Alps Mts.

Rhine

Corsica

Sardinia

Balearic Islands

Algiers

Pyrenees Mts.

Ebro R.

| | 250 | 500 | 750 Kilometers |
| 0 | 250 | 500 Miles |

Map 9

East and West: Ottomans in Europe

The Turkish people, led by the Ottomans, conquered the Byzantine Empire once and for all in 1453 with the capture of Constantinople. This was a tremendous victory and afterwards the Turks were on the move. They added vast tracts of lands to their wealthy empire. The Ottomans were very effective at getting the Europeans to accept them as an equal power. They had an intricate and effective government, with a strong and well-organized military. This exercise traces the growth of Ottoman strength and influence in Europe and the Mediterranean regions.

Locations

On Map 9 . . .

—Place the following names and dates alongside the appropriate battle symbols:

1. Vienna, 1683
2. Lepanto, 1571
3. Mohacs, 1526

—In the proper shaded regions, place the extent of Ottoman territorial gains in:

4. 1451
5. 1481
6. 1521
7. 1566

8. Also, label the territories lost to the Ottomans in 1699.

—Finally, label your map with the following regions:

9. Anatolia
10. Aragon
11. Moldavia
12. Papal States
13. Switzerland
14. Transylvania
15. Wallachia

Society and Civilizations

1.   After 1566, the northern boundaries of the Ottoman Empire were relatively fixed. What occurred to stop further movement into Northern Europe?

_____

_____

_____

_____

_____

_____

2.   What were the strengths and weaknesses of the Ottomans?

_____

_____

_____

_____

_____

_____

3.   How were these strengths and weakness linked to their territories?

_____

_____

_____

_____

_____

_____

4.   What were the long-term results of their conquests?

_____

_____

_____

_____

_____

_____

_____

Technology and Change: The Industrial Revolution

In the 18th century the economic and social structure of Europe was transformed. New forms and sources of energy and power, combined with an abandonment of traditional forms of labor, were the basis of the "Industrial Revolution." The Industrial Revolution changed society, families, culture and the economy in a myriad of ways.

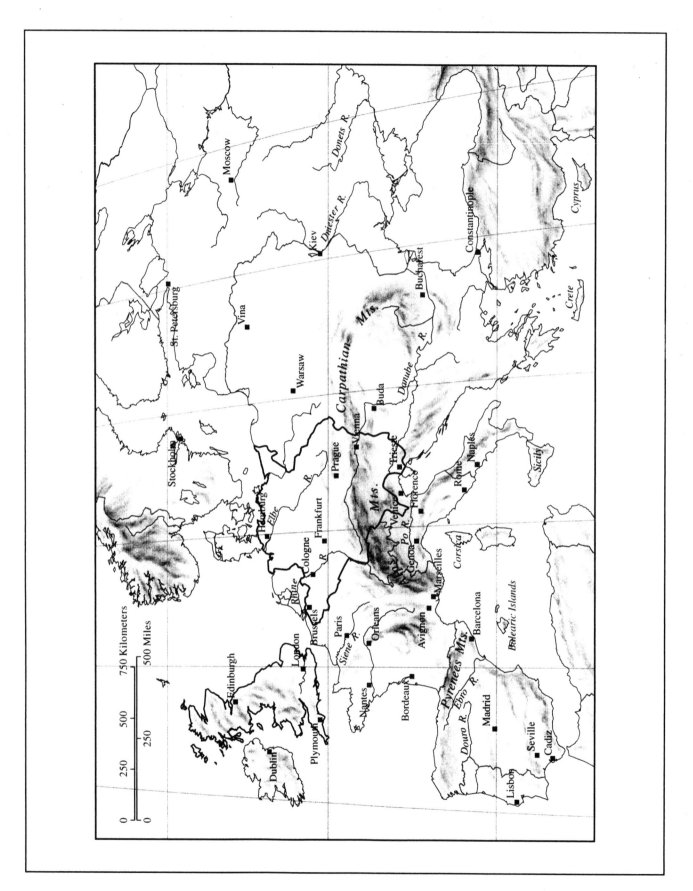

MAP 10

Locations

On Map 10 . . .

—Shade in the major manufacturing and industrial areas on the continent and Britain.

—In a different color, shade in or outline the areas on the continent and Britain that had developed railways by 1850.

Society and Environment

1.   Next to the following industries and sources of power, list the major associated regions.

Coal mining   _____

Iron industry   _____

Textile industry _____

Silk industry   _____

Banking   _____

2.   Name the three major centers on the continent where industrialization began.

_____

_____

_____

_____

3.   What was the foundation of the industrial revolution in Britain?

_____

_____

_____

_____

_____

4.   What were the environmental limitations on the development of the industrial revolution on the continent?

_____

_____

_____

_____

_____

5.   What were some of the environmental consequences of the industrial revolution on the continent? England?

_____

_____

_____

_____

_____

_____

6.   What were some of the social consequences of the industrial revolution on the continent? England?

_____

_____

_____

_____

_____

_____

Early Modern Europe: Test Your Knowledge

Link the following city or region name on the left with the material goods, event, or development most appropriate to it on the right:

Amsterdam	16th century inflation rate of foodstuffs
Belgium	Cotton spinning mills
England	Exploration of west coast of Africa
Holy Roman Empire	Francs Bacon's Scientific Method
Kensington, London	Industrial fair
Mediterranean	Industrial investment banking
Midlands, Britain	Overthrow of the Aztecs
Portugal	Saint Bartholomew's Day massacre
Spain	Stock exchange
Vassy, France	Thirty Years' War

Part Five: Europe in the Late 18th and 19th Centuries

Population and economic growth and rivalries characterized the European states of the eighteenth and early nineteenth centuries. These rivalries were not all played out on European territory. The main powers became very interested in the concept of a balance of power throughout the world. This meant they felt the need to limit the power of some states, and expand and support the power of others. The tools used for this process were mainly two: diplomacy and the military. Foreign ministries sprouted in far off places and the sizes of standing armies were increased. Maritime powers increased the sizes of their navies.

Revolutions and Ethnic Identities

Despite attempts to maintain the status quo, a new wave of revolution and reform spread across Europe in the second half of the nineteenth century. The 1830's to the 1850's saw revolts in Spain, Portugal, France, Italy, Germany, Russia and Poland. After the revolts generally ended in 1848, most of Europe suffered economic and political crises. France's government fell for the second time in a generation. Italy and Germany, on the other hand, were at last able to unify. Italy had not been a single state since the fall of the Roman Empire. At the same time, many dissatisfied people lived under the control of either the Austro-Hungarian or Russian Empire. Ethnic conflicts and the desire for self rule kept central and eastern Europe in turmoil, as it remains today.

The late eighteenth century saw two important revolutions in the west: the American Revolution[1] and the French Revolution. Both were the result of long term

---

[1]The revolution that freed North America had little immediate effect on the colonial status of countries in South and Central America. These lands remained in the hand of European powers into the nineteenth century. The Spanish and the Portuguese held these territories and were loath to give up their wealth, although their powers were weakening. Slowly the lands of South America demanded and got independence, despite the Spanish use of well-trained troops to crush the resistance.

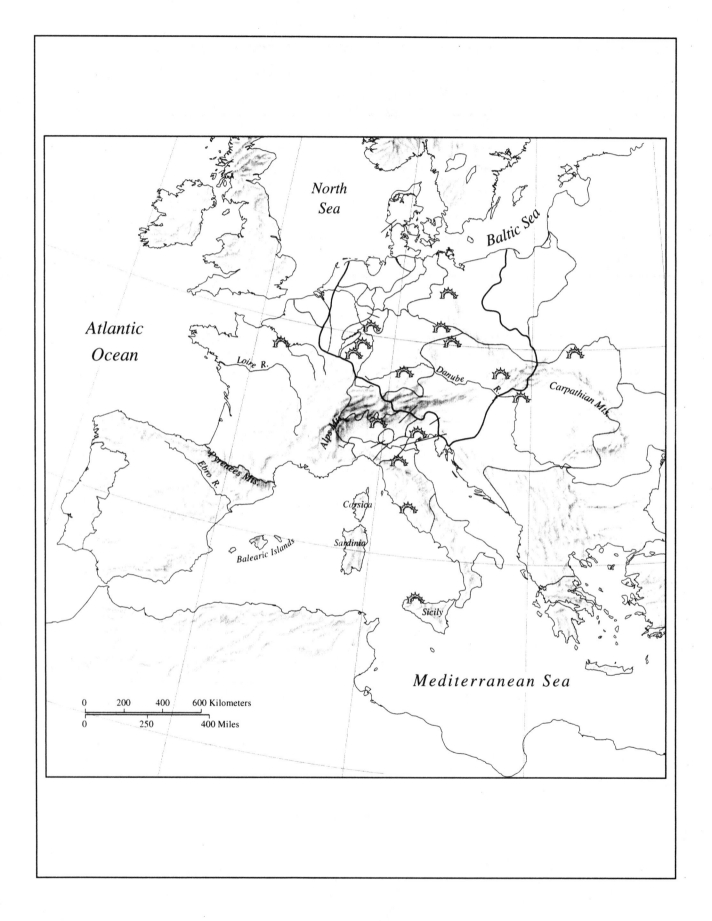

North
Sea

Baltic Sea

Atlantic
Ocean

Loire R.

Danube

R.

Carpathian Mts.

Pyrenees Mts.

Ebro R.

Alps Mts.

Corsica

Balearic Islands

Sardinia

Sicily

Mediterranean Sea

| 0 | 200 | 400 | 600 Kilometers |
| 0 | | 250 | 400 Miles |

MAP 11

problems. The French sought, like the Americans, to ground their constitution in the idea of equal rights. The implementation of equal rights was neither easy nor peaceful. Other European nations feared that violent upheaval would spread from France and, thus, an informal coalition formed against the French. In response, the French had built up a large and impressive army and conquered even the Netherlands. Terror, instability and confusion, however, soon dominated French politics and the economy, which led to the rise of Napoleon.

Revolutionary movements naturally occurred in tandem with nationalism. Nationalism was the direct result of a growing sense of ethnic or community identity that arose out of an increased awareness and interest in the study of local languages, architecture, art and history. Nationalistic ideals and ethnic identification, paradoxically, resulted in both a desire for political and cultural unity and the fragmentation of state structures—and, thus, revolts.

$\wp$

Locations

On Map 11 . . .

—Using different colors, lightly shade in and label the following root-language groups:

1. Slavic
2. Hellenic
3. Germanic
4. Celtic
5. Baltic
6. Latin

—Next, on the same map, using European revolts from between 1820 to 1849, place a minimum of 14 instances of revolts alongside the name of the city or state and the date.

States and Societies

1. Define self-determination. How is self determination related to the idea of Nationalism?

_____

_____

_____

_____

_____

_____

_____

2. Briefly outline the factors that led to the French revolution.

_____

_____

_____

_____

_____

_____

_____

3. Next, briefly outline the factors that led to the American revolution.

_____

_____

_____

_____

_____

_____

4. What impact did the independence movements in conquered territories (such as those in Asia, Africa, Latin America) have on Europe, and what impact did the revolutions in Europe have on these conquered lands?

_____

_____

_____

_____

_____

_____

_____

5. What factors led to the Franco-Prussian War and what were the results of the war on territorial boundaries in the region?

_____
_____
_____
_____
_____
_____

6. In essay form, briefly describe the factors the led to the rise of Napoleon. How did the rise of Napoleon Bonapart in France impact European politics and territorial boundaries?

_____
_____
_____
_____
_____
_____
_____
_____
_____
_____
_____
_____
_____
_____
_____
_____
_____
_____
_____
_____
_____
_____

Population Growth

Early in the eighteenth century, European countries began to experience a period of economic and demographic growth. Jackson Spielvogel estimated that the "total European population was around 120 million in 1700, [and] expanded to 140 million by 1750, and then grew to 190 million by 1790."[2]

℘

1. Describe the probable causes of the sudden population growth experienced in Europe.

_____
_____
_____
_____
_____
_____
_____

2. How did population growth affect the economy generally in European countries?

_____
_____
_____
_____
_____
_____
_____

3. How did population growth affect culture in European countries?

_____
_____
_____
_____
_____
_____
_____

---

[2]Jackson Spielvogel, 1997, *Western Civilization, Comprehensive Volume, Third Edition*. West Publishing Company, p. 654.

4. How did population growth affect the family and society in European countries?

_____

_____

_____

_____

_____

_____

_____

5. Where was the population concentrated and why?

_____

_____

_____

_____

_____

_____

_____

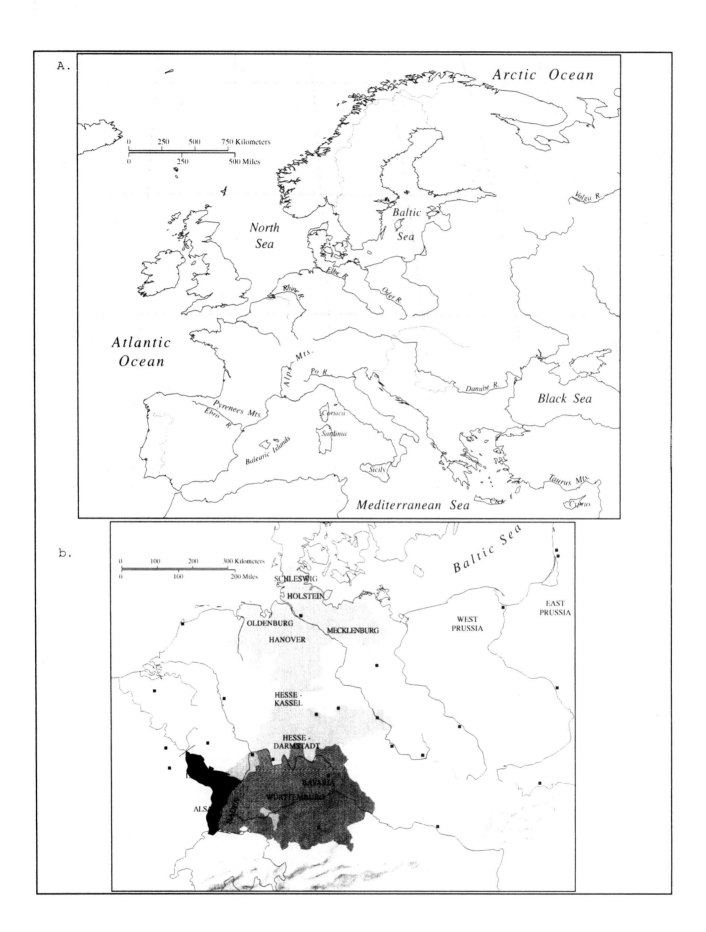

A.

Arctic Ocean

250 500 750 Kilometers

250 500 Miles

North Sea

Baltic Sea

Volga R.

Atlantic Ocean

Rhine R.

Elbe R.

Oder R.

Alps Mts.

Po R.

Danube R.

Black Sea

Pyrenees Mts.

Ebro R.

Corsica

Sardinia

Balearic Islands

Sicily

Taurus Mts.

Crete

Cyprus

Mediterranean Sea

b.

100 200 300 Kilometers

100 200 Miles

Baltic Sea

SCHLESWIG

HOLSTEIN

OLDENBURG

MECKLENBURG

WEST PRUSSIA

EAST PRUSSIA

HANOVER

HESSE - KASSEL

HESSE - DARMSTADT

BAVARIA

WÜRTTEMBURG

ALSACE

MAP 12

Europe on the Eve of World War I

The nineteenth and early twentieth centuries can be characterized as an age of imperialism. Powerful nations of the east and west dominated weaker and smaller states whenever and wherever possible. Europeans, for example, grabbed nearly all of Africa over the course of just a single generation, and carved it up among themselves without regard for traditional boundaries or ethnic relationships—even as Europeans themselves were increasingly interested in their own ethnic and cultural ties. On the continent, boundaries were in flux and imperialism was an attitude applied at home as well as abroad. The search for peace through a reorganization of states ultimately led to economic and political conflict rather than cooperation.

Locations

On the appropriate inset on Map 12, place the number of the following regions and dates of incorporation into Germany:

1. Alsace-Lorraine, after 1871

2. Baden

3. Bavaria, 1971

4. North German Confederation, 1866–67

5. Prussia, 1862

Also label the appropriate map with the following cities:

6.	Berlin	11.	Nuremberg
7.	Breslau	12.	Prague
8.	Cracow	13.	Trier
9.	Hamburg	14.	Verdun
10.	Munich	15.	Warsaw

On the other map, carefully draw in the boundaries of, and label, the following states in Europe as of 1871:

16.	Austria	21.	Hungary	26.	Norway
17.	Belgium	22.	Italy	27.	Portugal
18.	Bulgaria	23.	Macedonia	28.	Serbia
19.	France	24.	Montenegro/Albania	29.	Spain
20.	Greece	25.	Netherlands	30.	Sweden

States and Civilizations

1.   Describe the characteristics and results of the "Bismarckian System."

_____
_____
_____
_____
_____
_____
_____

2.   What effect did the Congress of Berlin have on the territorial possessions of the Ottomans, Bulgaria, and Russia?

_____
_____
_____
_____
_____
_____
_____

3.   Describe the reasons for British concerns over Germany in the late 19th century.

_____
_____
_____
_____
_____
_____
_____

4.   Briefly describe the "Bosnian Crisis of 1908–1909."

_____
_____
_____
_____
_____
_____
_____

Europe in the Late 18th and 19th Centuries:
Test Your Knowledge

Create a chart chronology of 19th-century Western history using the following selection of dates and events.

Events

Anti-socialist Law	Revolt in the Austrian Empire
Belgian revolt	Revolts in southern Italy
Belgium establishes settlements in Congo	and Sardinia crushed
British expeditionary force in Egypt	Second Napoleonic Empire
Crimean War	
Danish War	**Dates**
Darwin postulates Theory of Organic Evolution	1821
Decemberist revolt (Russia)	1825
Dominion of Canada formed	1830
Dreyfus affair (France)	1838
Emancipation of serfs (Russia)	1848
Emancipation of slaves (United States)	1852
First Zionist Congress	1854–56
Franco-Prussian War	1859
German Empire proclaimed	1861
German revolution	1863
Italy annexes Rome	1864
July revolution (France)	1867
June days workers' revolt (France)	1870
Kingdom of Italy is proclaimed	1870–71
Paris commune	1871
Pasteurization invented	1876
Polish uprising	1878
Publication of *A Doll's House*, by H. Ibsen	1882
Publication of the *Communist Manifesto* by Marx	1884
Reform Act of William Gladstone (Britain)	1895–99
Republican constitution (Third Republic, France)	1897

Part Six: Europe in the 20th Century

In the latter years of the nineteenth century, European states turned again to overseas expansion and imperialism became a defining characteristic of the time. Since the Americas were lost to them, Asia and Africa attracted the attentions of the European states. Although they were not able to dominate the territories in Asia and Africa quite as successfully as they had dominated colonies in previous centuries, nevertheless these new colonies provided immediate benefits, both material and social, and proved worth the trouble. The European powers acquired some territories outright; others came under their strong influence. The United States expressed interest in the Pacific Rim countries and claimed territories. Western people generally believed themselves superior to the Asian and African people, and justified their imperialism by pointing to the mutual benefit of such oppression. Kipling's poem the "White Man's Burden" exemplifies this western feeling of superiority.

Europe to the Mid-Twentieth Century

World War I was one of the defining events of the twentieth century. The brutality, overwhelming scope, length of the war, and its final settlement would prepare the road for yet another major conflict. Its destructiveness was a shock and disappointment to Europeans—intellectual, industrial worker, and farmer alike. The precipitating events resulted from conflict in the Balkans. Austrians had held Bosnia and Herzegovina under their protection until 1908 when the states were formally annexed. The Serbs, their hopes for a larger Serbian kingdom dashed, helped precipitate an international incident in response to Austrian actions. In 1912, more attention was drawn to the region when the Ottoman Turks were defeated in the First Balkan war. New divisions of territories resulted. In 1913, another Balkans war produced further divisions of the Balkans. Not surprisingly, therefore, the conflict known as the "Great War" was ignited by a confrontation between Austria and Serbia, after the heir to the Austrian throne was assassinated in Sarajevo, a Bosnian city.

The end of World War I meant the redrawing of European and world boundaries. At the Paris Peace Conference, the losers were disarmed and forced to pay reparations, but they also lost territory and colonies. In central and Eastern Europe, some of the most

74

profound rearrangements of people and states took place. Germany was severely punished for its role in the "Great War" and Germans would come to resent their punishments deeply.

Still, in 1919, Europeans were optimistic, despite early signs of serious economic trouble—the Great Depression would soon hit. The Germans were deeply affected by economic setbacks and were plunged into poverty. They soon came to resent their position in the post-war world. According to a contemporary observer, Heinrich Hauser, "An almost unbroken chain of homeless men extends the whole length of the great Hamburg-Berlin highway. . . ."

Only twenty years passed before the next major conflagration would occur. The depressed economy would help precipitate non-democratic political solutions to economic problems as well as offer opportunities for the creation of authoritarian and totalitarian states. World War II was inevitable when one such power, the Nazi party, ignited a form of German nationalism that proclaimed, among other things, a need for more living space (*lebensraum*). Again, a massively destructive war was fought on European soil, with devastating demographic, material and psychological results.

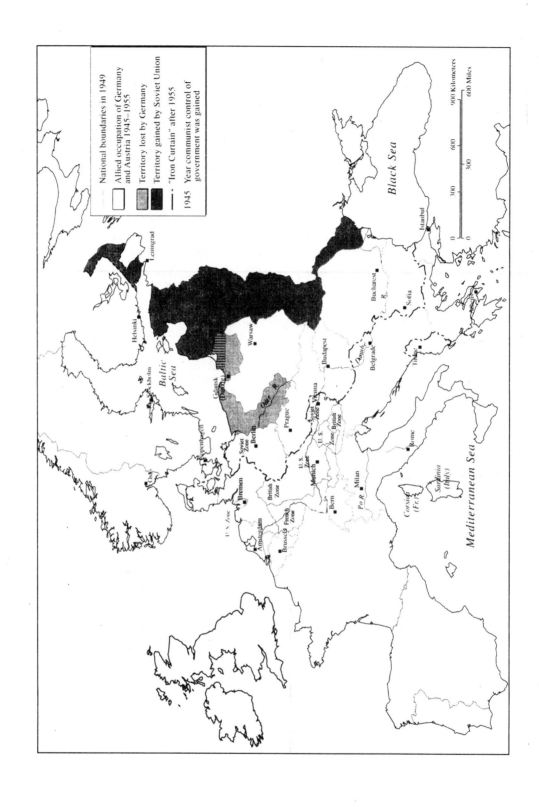

National boundaries in 1949

Allied occupation of Germany and Austria 1945–1955

Territory lost by Germany

Territory gained by Soviet Union

1945   "Iron Curtain" after 1955

Year communist control of government was gained

Black Sea

Baltic Sea

Mediterranean Sea

Leningrad

Helsinki

Stockholm

Oslo

Copenhagen

Gdansk (Danzig)

Warsaw

Berlin

Prague

Soviet Zone

British Zone

U. S. Zone

French Zone

Bremen

Amsterdam

Brussels

Munich

Bern

Milan

Vienna

Soviet Zone

U. S. Zone

British Zone

Budapest

Belgrade

Bucharest

Sofia

Istanbul

Rome

Corsica (Fr.)

Sardinia (Italy)

Oder R.

Danube

Po R.

Tiber

300   600   900 Kilometers

300   600 Miles

Locations

On Map 13 . . .

—Place or label the following locations:

1.	Albania	6.	Estonia	11.	Lithuania
2.	Austria	7.	Greece	12.	Poland
3.	Belgium	8.	Hungary	13.	Romania
4.	Bulgaria	9.	Italy	14.	White Russia
5.	Czechoslovakia	10.	Latvia	15.	Yugoslavia

—Next, using different colors, carefully indicate the regions which were:

16. NATO members
17. NATO allies
18. Warsaw Pact members

—Finally, using symbols or numbers, indicate on your map the major distribution of military installations in the 1950s and 1960s:

19.	Soviet naval ports	23.	US nuclear missile submarines
20.	Warsaw pact missile bases	24.	Soviet nuclear missle submarines
21.	NATO missile bases	25.	US troops
22.	US naval ports		

World War II

1.   Why do many scholars believe that the Spanish Civil war was essentially the first battle of W.W.II? What issues were at stake? Who won?

_____

_____

_____

_____

_____

_____

_____

_____

_____

_____

2.   By what means did the Nazis come to power in Germany? What were their original goals?

_____

_____

_____

_____

_____

_____

_____

3.   Describe the resistance movements to the Nazis. What accounts for their failures?

_____

_____

_____

_____

_____

_____

_____

4.   Summarize the main objectives of the League of Nations. Why was the League deemed a failure?

_____

_____

_____

_____

_____

_____

5.   Summarize the positions outlined in President Wilson's Fourteen Points. What was his primary goal? What were the problems with his plans?

_____

_____

_____

_____

_____

_____

6. Why were nationalism and militarism popular prior to W.W.II in Japan? Why, in particular, was democracy denounced?

_____

_____

_____

_____

_____

7. What factors in China prevented the Chinese from stopping Japanese aggression in Manchuria?

_____

_____

_____

_____

_____

8. What were the Japanese goals in Asia?

_____

_____

_____

_____

_____

Post Cold-War Europe

Most of Africa, Asia and Latin America emerged from World War II as numerous independent states. The independence of these new nations, however, offered ideological and economic battle grounds for the cold war "superpowers," the United States and Soviet Union. Regional developments, such as those in Cuba, Angola, Korea and Vietnam had global repercussions as east and west vied for power, economic advantage and military superiority. Smaller nations learned to use the cold war atmosphere for economic gain and sometimes, political clout far outreaching the size and wealth of their populations.

With the collapse of the Soviet Union, newly independent states emerged in central and eastern Europe. The Soviet republics, one by one, declared their independent status. The rapid, quite dramatic, collapse of the eastern superpower has left much of the world in confusion. The loss of this monolithic, unified political system has allowed ethnic conflicts to threaten and take lives and property. The long term impact of this global change will not be known for decades, perhaps centuries, to come.

1.   In which European and Eastern European areas did the US pursue active intervention? What, theoretically, motivated this intervention? Were US goals achieved? Why or why not?

_____

_____

_____

_____

_____

_____

2.   During the cold war, which nations chose non-alignment and for what reasons? What were the advantages and disadvantages of non-alignment? In particular, what role did the new communist China play in the cold war?

_____

_____

_____

_____

_____

_____

Boundaries and Borders: Changes in the Later 20th Century

World War II had a profound impact in the territories influenced and claimed by the European powers in Africa, Asia, and the Middle East. The colonies made claims for independence and enthusiastically embraced nationalistic movements. India and Pakistan freed themselves from British rule, and other Asian countries also managed to loosen the bonds of European control. In the Middle East, the growing nationalism of the Arab states helped put an end to colonial control, but they were unable to prevent the creation of a new Jewish state, Israel.

Crises in the Balkans continue to occur. Soon after the collapse of the Soviet Union, the Yugoslavian political scene began to fragment. The republics began to lobby for more independence, which ultimately led to war after negotiations failed. More than one quarter of a million people have been killed in the brutal separatist struggles and at least 2 million others have been displaced. The long-term results of the peace treaty resulting from the 1995 Dayton accords remain to be seen.

In the twentieth century, we have seen technological advances, a growing desire among many people for economic and political independence, and the overthrow of old monarchical and colonial forms of government.

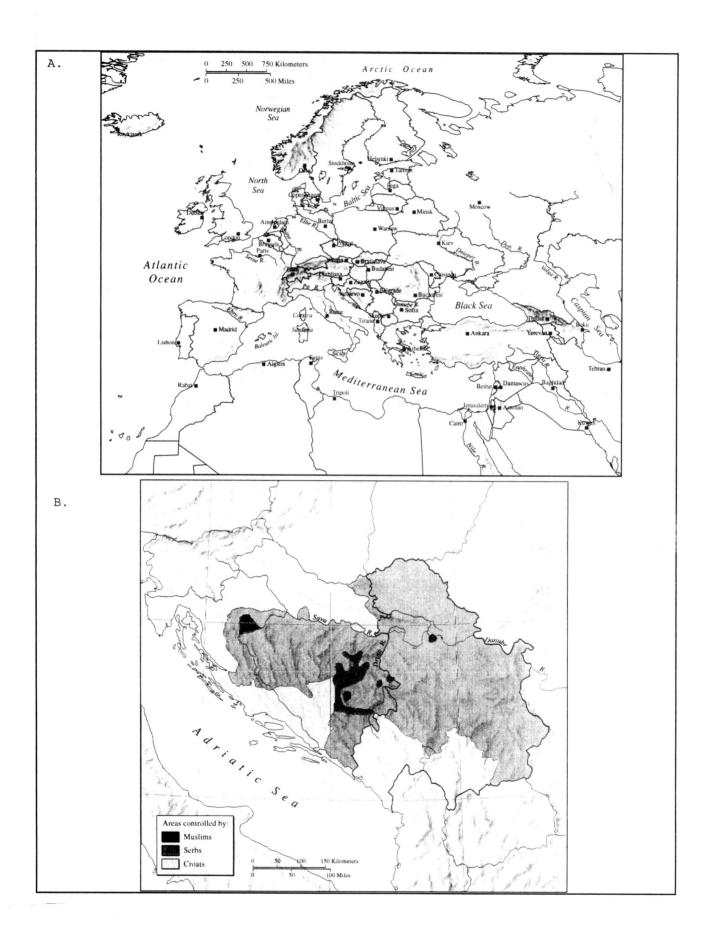

A.

B.

Areas controlled by:
Muslims
Serbs
Croats

MAP 14

Locations

—On the appropriate map, locate the following states in their post cold war boundaries:

1. Austria
2. Belarus
3. Bulgaria
4. Czech Republic
5. Germany
6. Hungary
7. Moldovia
8. Romania
9. Slovakia
10. Ukraine

—On the other map, locate the following lands and sectors of the former Yugoslavia, as of 1995:

11. Albania
12. Croatia
13. Federation of Bosnia and Herzegovina
14. French sector
15. Former Yugoslav Republic of Macedonia
16. NATO forces
17. Slovenia
18. US sector
19. Yugoslavia
20. Indicate any post-1995 territorial changes with dates and regions clearly marked

—Place the following cities on the Yugoslav map:

21. Banja Luka
22. Belgrade
23. Mostar
24. Novi Sad
25. Pec
26. Skopje
27. Split
28. Srebenica
29. Tuzla
30. Zagreb

Territory, States, and the End of the Cold War

1.   Write a short essay discussing the territorial and social problems that have arisen because of the fall of the Soviet Union? In particular, consider major political and boundary changes in eastern European and Asian states.

_____

_____

_____

_____

_____

_____

_____

_____

_____

_____

_____

_____

_____

_____

_____

_____

_____

_____

_____

_____

_____

_____

_____

_____

_____

_____

_____

_____

_____

_____

_____

_____

_____

_____

2.   Write an essay comparing and contrasting the factors that led to the Russian Revolution and the beginning of the 20th century with the factors that led to the dissolution of the Soviet Union at the end on the 20th century.

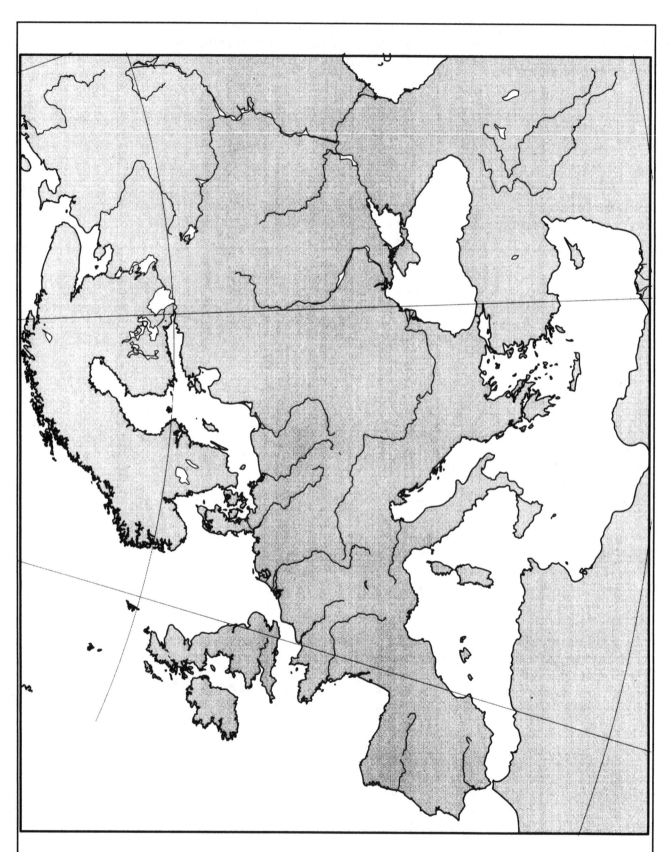

EUROPE

Europe in the Twentieth Century: Test Your Imagination

You have seen state boundaries change continually over time. This is an exercise of your imagination. On Map 15, draw the boundaries of Europe as you believe they will be fifty years from today. Mark on your map major changes in population that you foresee. Do you believe there will be any major wars on the order of the first and second world wars? Why or why not? What effect will the current Balkan crisis have in the long run?

Next, justify your predictions. Why do you believe the changes you suggest will occur? Use both current and past events to support your position.

_____

_____

_____

_____

_____

_____

_____

_____

_____

_____

_____

_____

_____

_____

_____

_____

_____

_____

_____

_____

_____

_____

_____

_____

_____

Extra Maps

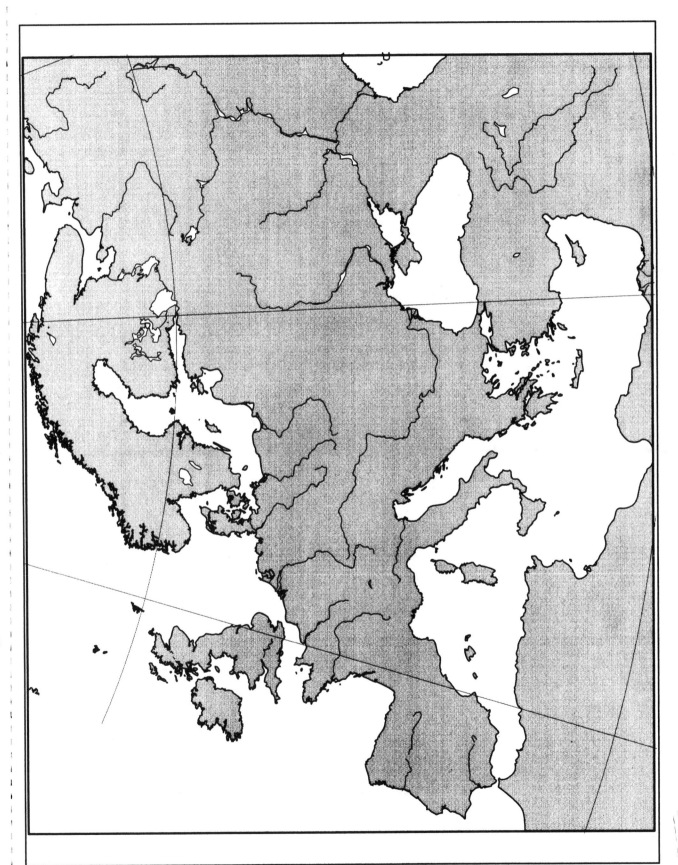

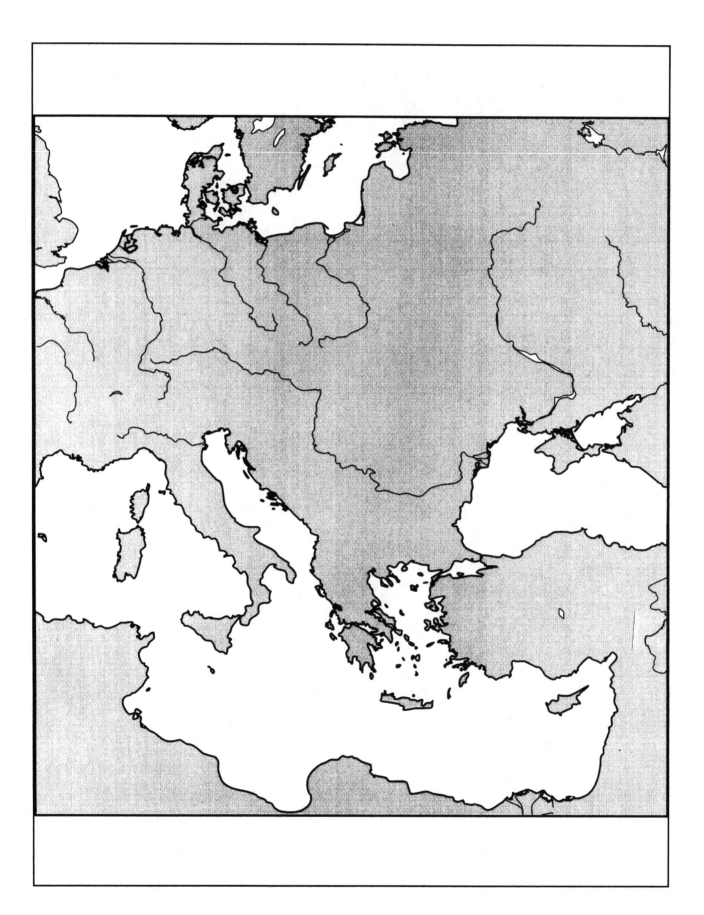

CENTRAL EUROPE

MEDITERRANEAN

Notes